The Conflict Resolution Library™

Dealing with Choices

• Elizabeth Vogel •

The Rosen Publishing Group's
PowerKids Press™
New York

For Mom and Dad

Published in 2000 by The Rosen Publishing Group, Inc.
29 East 21st Street, New York, NY 10010

Copyright © 2000 by The Rosen Publishing Group, Inc.

Photo Illustrations by Debra L. Rothenberg

First Edition

Layout and design: Erin McKenna

Vogel, Elizabeth.
    Dealing with choices / by Elizabeth Vogel.
            p.   cm. — (The conflict resolution library)
    Includes index.
      ISBN 0-8239-5410-2
    1. Choice (Psychology) 2. Decision-making. I. Title. II. Series.
    BF611.V63 1999
    153.8'3—dc21   98-51675
                                                                                                          CIP

Manufactured in the United States of America

Contents

What Are Choices?

Have you ever had to make a **difficult** choice? Having choices means having to select one thing instead of another. You might have one choice to make, or many. Having a choice can be exciting and **confusing** at the same time. When you have to make a **decision**, you might feel grown-up. Sometimes the choice seems easy, other times a decision can be hard to make. There are things you can do to help you make the best choice possible. The more you know about your choices, the easier it will be to make a decision.

◀ *It can be hard to make a choice. Sometimes it may seem as if you want everything at once.*

Making Decisions

Do you have a decision to make right now? When you were younger, someone else, like your parents or another **trusted** adult, made decisions for you. Now that you are older, you have your own decisions to make. There are many different kinds of decisions. Maybe you are deciding on what color winter jacket to wear. Maybe you have a much bigger decision to make, like where you want to go to camp this summer. It is important to learn how to make decisions because you will have more to make as you continue to grow.

Parents can help you make a decision like which winter jacket to buy. ▶

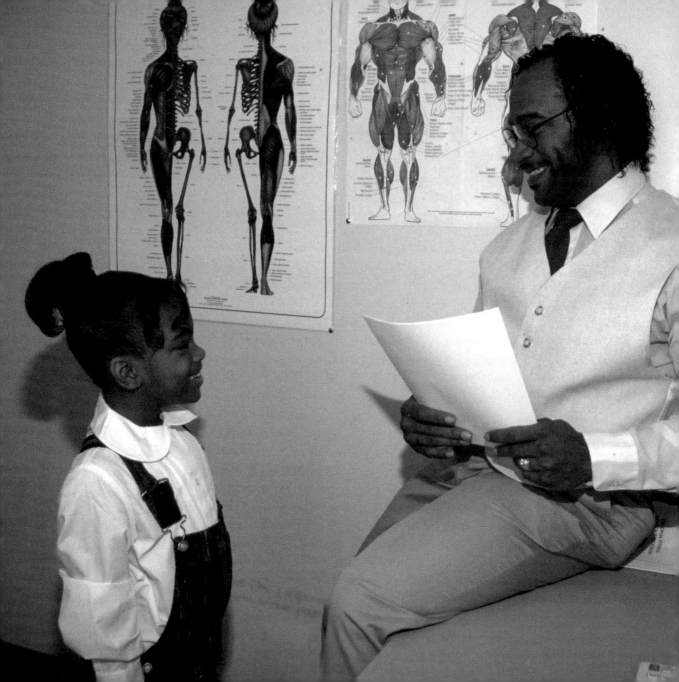

Talking to Adults

Parents, guardians, older **siblings**, baby-sitters, and teachers can help you make difficult decisions. They have had many years of **experience** making choices. Maybe your mother knows which choice will be better for you because she once had to make a similar decision. Maybe your teacher knows a lot about after-school activities and can help you pick the ones that are best for you. Asking adults for help in making choices is a good idea. You might find out some very useful **information**.

◀ *A teacher can help you with the choices you have to make.*

Sam's Choice

Sam is very confused. He doesn't know which after-school activity to choose. His friend David plays football, Dawn takes French lessons, and Dwayne likes to sing with the school chorus. Sam doesn't know which one is right for him. He asks his friends, but he is still not sure. Then his mom suggests that he try each one for a day. Sam went with each friend to try their activities. After trying them all, Sam knew he was happiest playing football after school. Sam felt good about his choice and the way he reached his decision.

Trying different activities can help you find out which one you like the best. ▶

Talking to Friends

Your friends can help you make an important decision. Chances are your friends have begun to have a lot of different experiences. Maybe they've already gone to the camp you're thinking of attending this summer. Are you deciding on which instrument to play in school? Your friend might know about the violin or maybe he has played the piano for years. Your friends can be great **sources** of information. Don't be shy about asking them questions. They might be able to help you make a good choice.

◀ *Tim helped Rob choose the violin.*
He knew Rob would love it.

Maisy's Birthday

Maisy's birthday is coming soon and she wants to have a party. Her mom said she has three kinds of parties to choose from. The choices are a pottery party, an ice-skating party, or a dance party. All of them sound great, so Maisy doesn't know which one to choose.

Maisy talked to her friend Gina. Gina said the pottery party would be fun. Plus, everyone would go home with a pottery mug they made at the party. Maisy agreed that these were good reasons, so she chose the pottery party.

Talking with a friend about a tough choice is one good way to make a decision. ▶

Other Ways to Choose

There are different ways to make decisions. Sometimes it's helpful to make a list. Write the things you like about a choice on one side of a piece of paper. Then write what you don't like about the choice on the other side. When you are finished, look at both sides. The choice with the best things wins.

Another idea is to go to your local library. Look for books on the subject you are thinking about. Reading a good book with lots of facts can also help you make a decision.

◀ *Writing down the good and bad things about your choice can help you make a decision.*

How Do You Feel?

How do you feel after you've made a choice? You might have a lot of different **emotions**. Are you worried that you chose the wrong thing? This is okay, but it is important not to worry too much. Most choices do not last forever. Maybe you thought about trying out for the school play, but chose not to. Perhaps you felt badly when you watched the play. Remember, there will be another play next year. Even if you feel like you made the wrong choice, something good might come out of it. You can always learn from the choices that you make.

Sometimes, making the wrong choice can help you learn about what's right for you. ▶

Jeremy's Friends

Jeremy's family planned a trip to an amusement park. Jeremy was allowed to choose one friend to go with him. His friend Adam was very popular and fun, but Matthew was also Jeremy's friend. Matthew was a little shy, but Jeremy liked spending time with him. Jeremy didn't know which friend to take. Then he remembered that he took Adam on the last family trip. Maybe it was time to take another friend. When Jeremy asked Matthew to go to the park with him, Matthew was so happy. Jeremy knew he had made the right choice.

◀ *Jeremy knows that taking turns is a good way to make a choice.*

21

You Can Do It!

Having choices can be hard. You know to ask questions when talking to friends or adults in your life. You know you can make a list of the good and bad reasons to choose something. The more information you have about a choice the better the decision you make. It isn't easy being **responsible** for making decisions. Sometimes you will make great choices, and sometimes you might not. With each choice you make, you can learn more about what you like and dislike. This will help you as you continue to face choices throughout your life.

Glossary

confusing (kun-FYOO-zing) When something is hard to understand.

decision (dih-SIH-zhun) To make up your mind about something.

difficult (DIH-fuh-cult) When something is hard to do or hard to deal with.

emotions (ih-MOH-shunz) Strong feelings, such as anger or sadness.

experience (ik-SPIR-ee-ents) Knowledge or skill gained by doing or seeing things.

information (in-for-MAY-shun) Things known, facts.

responsible (rih-SPON-sih-bul) Being the one to take care of someone or something.

siblings (SIH-blingz) Sisters or brothers.

source (SORSS) Where something comes from.

trust (TRUST) To be able to depend on someone.

Index